UNDERSTAND YOUR Mind AND Body

Vision Loss

Hannalora Leavitt and Sarah Harvey

Explore other books at:
WWW.ENGAGEBOOKS.COM

VANCOUVER, B.C.

WWW.ENGAGEBOOKS.COM

Vision Loss: Understand Your Mind and Body
Leavitt, Hannalora -
Harvey, Sarah 1950 –
Text © 2023 Engage Books
Design © 2023 Engage Books

Edited by: A.R. Roumanis Ashley Lee,
Melody Sun, and Sarah Harvey
Design by: Mandy Christiansen

Text set in Montserrat Regular.
Chapter headings set in Hobgoblin.

FIRST EDITION / FIRST PRINTING

This book is not meant to replace the advice of a medical professional or be a tool for diagnosis. It is an educational tool to help children understand what they or other people are going through.

LIBRARY AND ARCHIVES CANADA CATALOGUING IN PUBLICATION

Title: Vision Loss: Understand Your Mind and Body Level 3 reader / Leavitt, Hannalora
Names: Leavitt, Hannalora, - author, Harvey, Sarah 1950 - author

Identifiers: Canadiana (print) 20200308874 | Canadiana (ebook) 20200308912
ISBN 978-1-77476-788-7 (hardcover)
ISBN 978-1-77476-789-4 (softcover)
ISBN 978-1-77476-791-7 (pdf)
ISBN 978-1-77476-790-0 (epub)
ISBN 978-1-77878-115-5 (audio)

Subjects:
LCSH: Vision Loss—Juvenile literature.
LCSH: Vision Loss in children—Juvenile literature.

Classification: LCC BF723.A4 J66 2023 | DDC J152.4/7—DC23

This project has been made possible in part by the Government of Canada.

Canada 🍁

Contents

What Is Vision Loss?

Vision loss affects a person's sense of sight. It can be in one eye or both eyes. Some people only lose a small part of their vision. Other people lose a lot. Most people who are **legally blind** are able to see a little bit.

KEY WORD

Legally blind: someone whose vision is at least ten times worse than someone with normal vision.

Only 15 percent of people with vision loss cannot see anything.

Vision loss can happen quickly. Sudden blurry vision, pain, or flashes of light can mean serious vision problems. Vision loss can also happen over a long period of time. Many people get eye diseases as they get older.

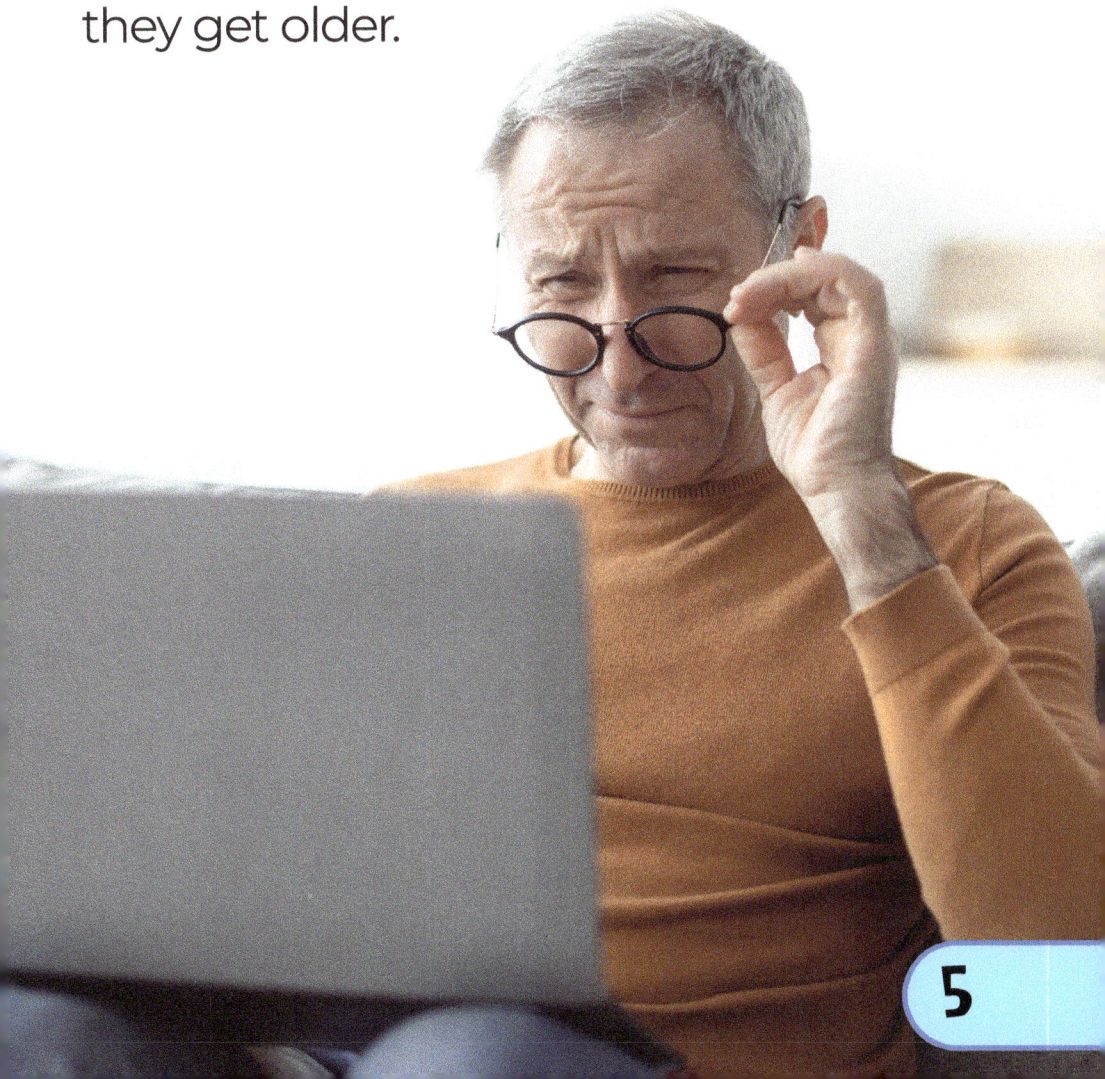

What Causes Vision Loss?

Some people are born blind. Others get vision problems later in life. Vision problems often run in families. They can also be caused by **injuries**.

KEY WORD

Injuries: harm or damage to the body.

Disorders or diseases of the eye can often change how people see. One of the most common causes of blindness is cataracts. A cataract is when part of the eye is cloudy. It often happens as people get older.

More than half of people over the age of 80 have cataracts or have had surgery to fix their cataracts.

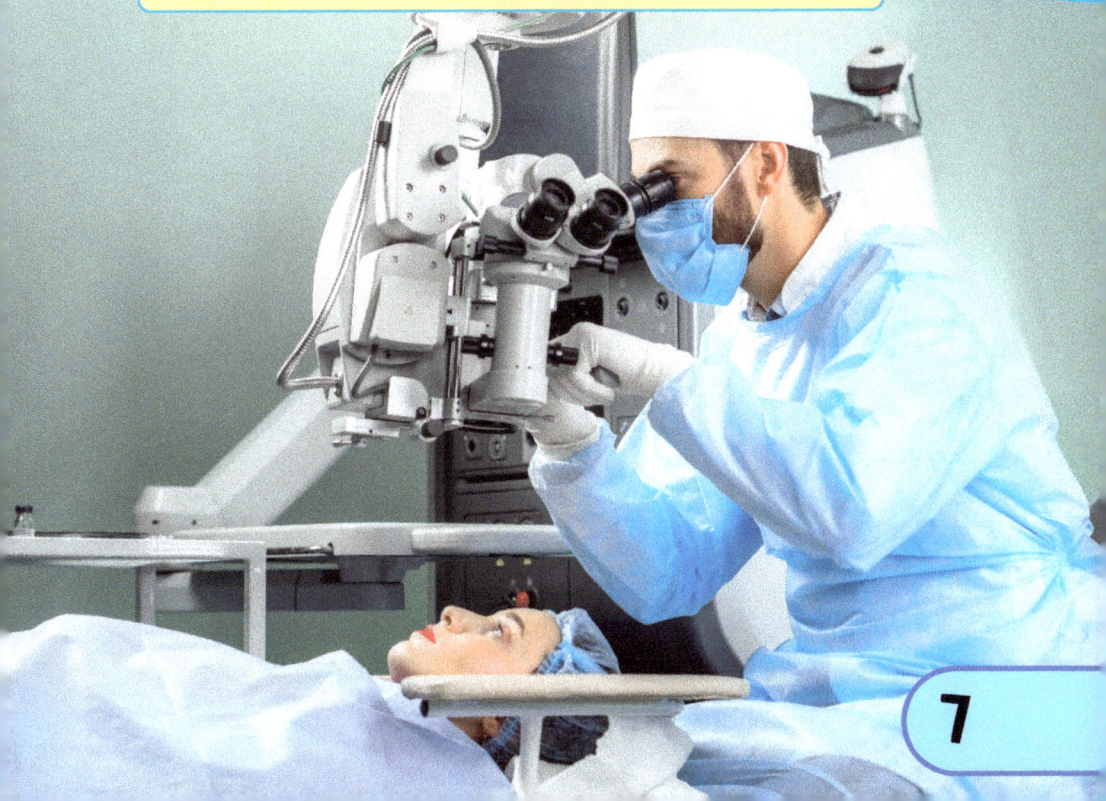

How Does Vision Loss Affect Your Brain?

The **occipital cortex** is the part of the brain that helps people understand what they see. It can change in people who become blind at a young age. It changes to help people better understand sound or what they are touching instead.

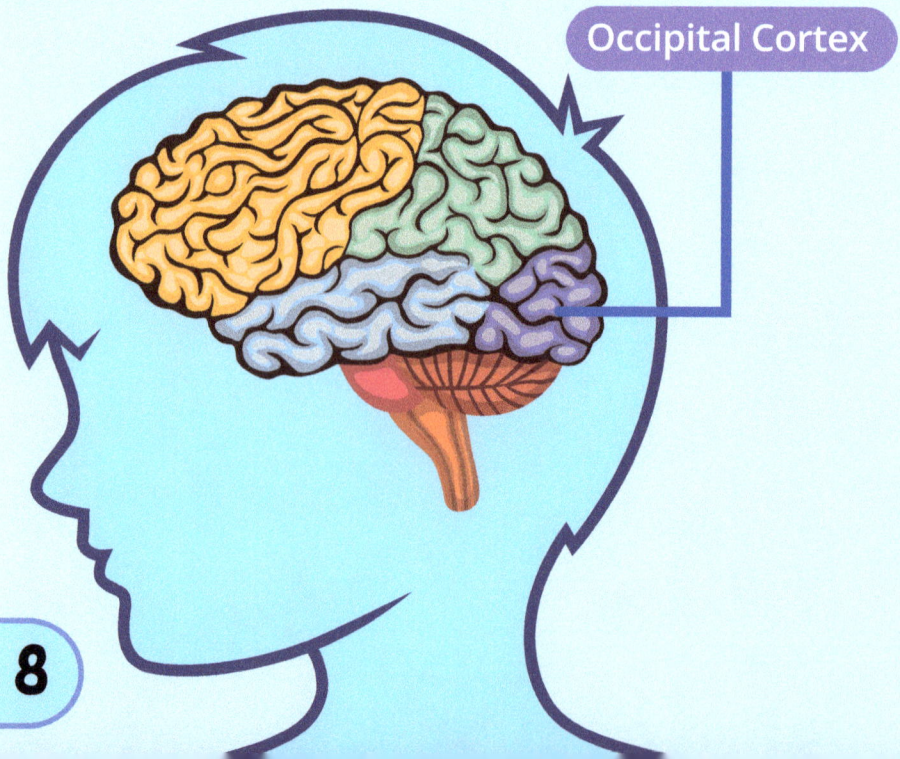

Occipital Cortex

Blurry vision can cause the brain to work harder to figure out what someone is seeing. This can lead to problems with memory or finding the right words to say. This is most common with older people.

How Does Vision Loss Affect Your Body?

Some people with vision loss do not get enough exercise. It is hard for someone to run or play sports if they cannot see properly. Not getting enough exercise can cause heart problems or **obesity**.

KEY WORD

Obesity: weighing more than what is healthy for a person's age and height.

Many older adults who have vision loss walk into objects they cannot see. Sometimes they cannot see how far down a step is. This causes them to fall and hurt themselves. These injuries may be bad and need to be seen by a doctor right away.

Older people with vision loss are two times more likely to fall than those without vision loss.

What Is it Like to Have Vision Loss?

People with vision loss can live full and active lives. They may need to learn new skills to help them do activities they enjoy. Some people with vision loss learn to walk using a cane or a **guide dog**.

KEY WORD

Guide dog: a dog that is trained to guide people with vision loss so they can walk safely.

Many people with vision loss learn to read **braille**. They may also learn to use a cell phone using voice commands. The person says what they want the phone to do and the phone will hear them.

KEY WORD

Braille: a way of writing things using raised dots that people read with their fingertips.

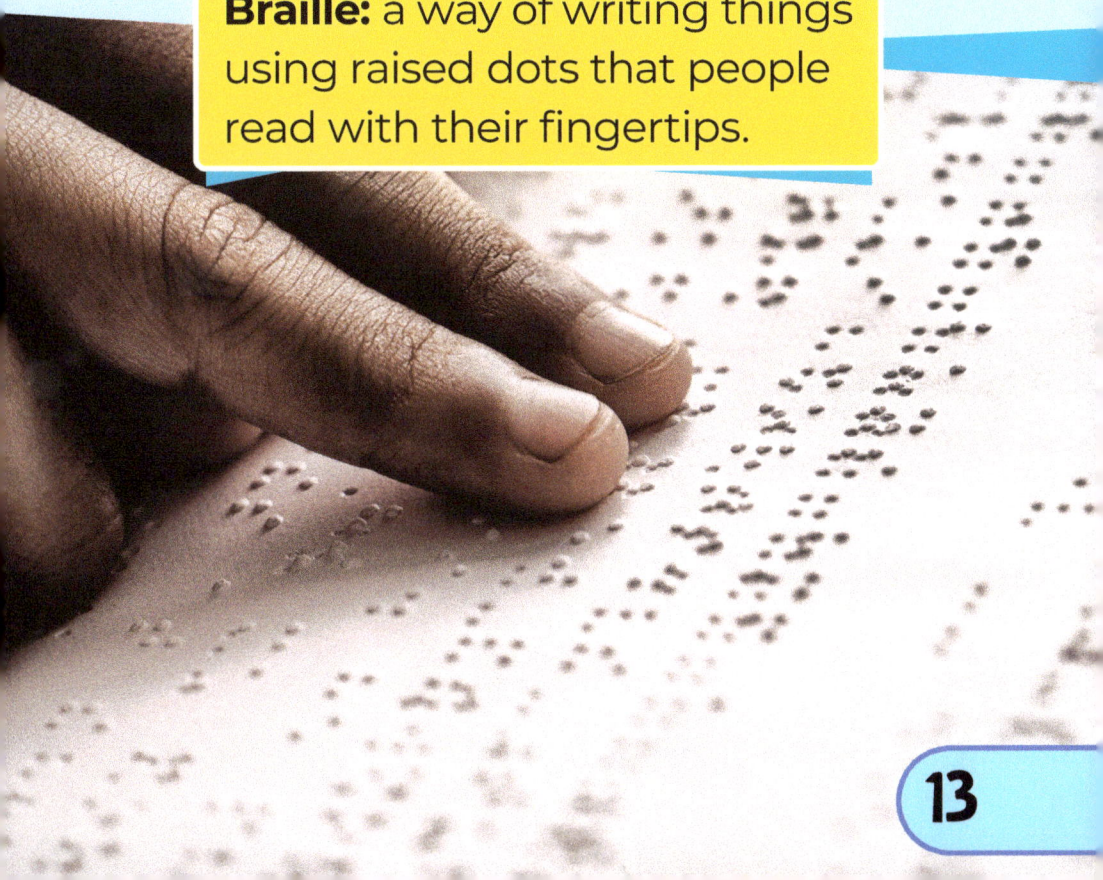

Does Vision Loss Last Forever?

About 80 percent of vision loss can be **prevented** or helped. Disorders of the retina are the most common cause of vision loss that lasts forever. The retina is a part of the eye that sends messages to the brain about the light it sees.

KEY WORD

Prevented: stopped from happening.

Most people with vision loss can be helped. People who have lost a lot of their vision may need to take medicine or have surgery. People who have only lost a small part of their vision can be helped by wearing glasses or **contact lenses**.

KEY WORD

Contact lenses: a thin piece of plastic that covers the eye to help make a person's vision better.

More than 140 million people around the world wear contact lenses.

Asking for Help

Asking for help can be hard. You may want to do everything yourself. Asking for help when you need it shows that you value yourself and trust others.

"I'm having a hard time reading my schoolwork. I've never had this problem before. What should I do?"

"I can't see as far as the other kids in my class. Can you take me to see an eye doctor?"

"Can you help me make the words on this screen bigger so I can read on my own?"

How to Help Others With Vision Loss

If you know someone with vision loss, remember to be patient. Many of them have to learn to do things differently. Here are some ways you can help them.

Ask before offering help
People with vision loss often do not need help from other people to do simple tasks. Many people like to do things on their own if they can. Always ask if someone needs help before helping them.

Be a good listener

If you know someone with vision loss, be a good listener. Do not speak over them. It is important for them to feel heard and to know you support them.

Do not pet guide dogs

If someone is walking with a guide dog, do not pet it. It is working. Petting it can make it lose focus. This can cause problems for the person it is guiding.

In 2021, there were more than 22,000 guide dogs working all over the world.

The History of Vision Loss

Valentin Haüy opened the first school for the blind in Paris sometime between 1784 and 1786. It was called the National Institute for Blind Youth. It only had twelve students when it opened.

Louis Braille lost his vision when he was three years old. He invented braille in 1824 when he was 15 years old. He even figured out how to write music using braille.

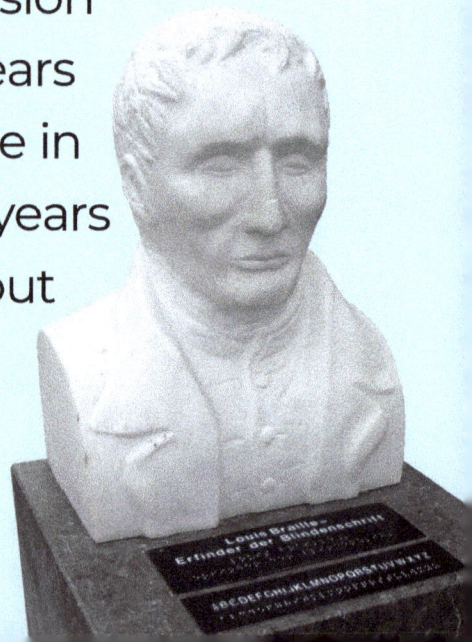

The discovery of **vaccines** and new medicines in the early 1900s helped doctors cure many of the causes of vision loss. Surgeries improved too. Scientists also came up with new tools to help doctors learn more about the eye and vision problems.

KEY WORD

Vaccines: a kind of medicine that stops people from getting sick.

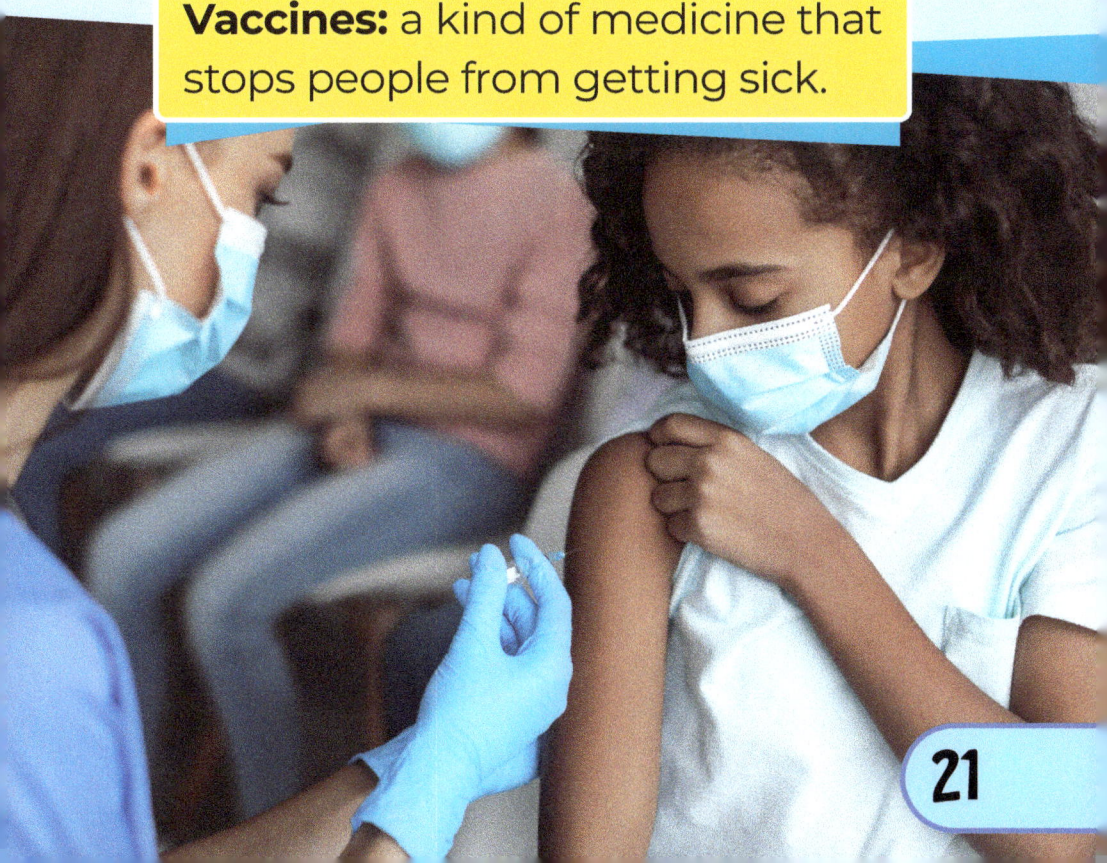

Vision Loss Superheroes

People with vision loss are able to do just about anything sighted people can do. Here are some people with vision loss who have done great things.

Erik Weihenmayer was the first blind person to reach the top of Mount Everest. By 2008, he had climbed the Seven Summits. These are the highest points on each continent.

Dame Judi Dench is a famous British actor. In 2012, she said that she has vision loss in both eyes. She continues to act in movies. She can no longer read. Family and friends read her lines to her.

Stevie Wonder has been blind since shortly after his birth. The singer-songwriter has won 25 Grammy Awards and one Academy Award. He has done a lot of work to make sure people with vision loss can live normal lives.

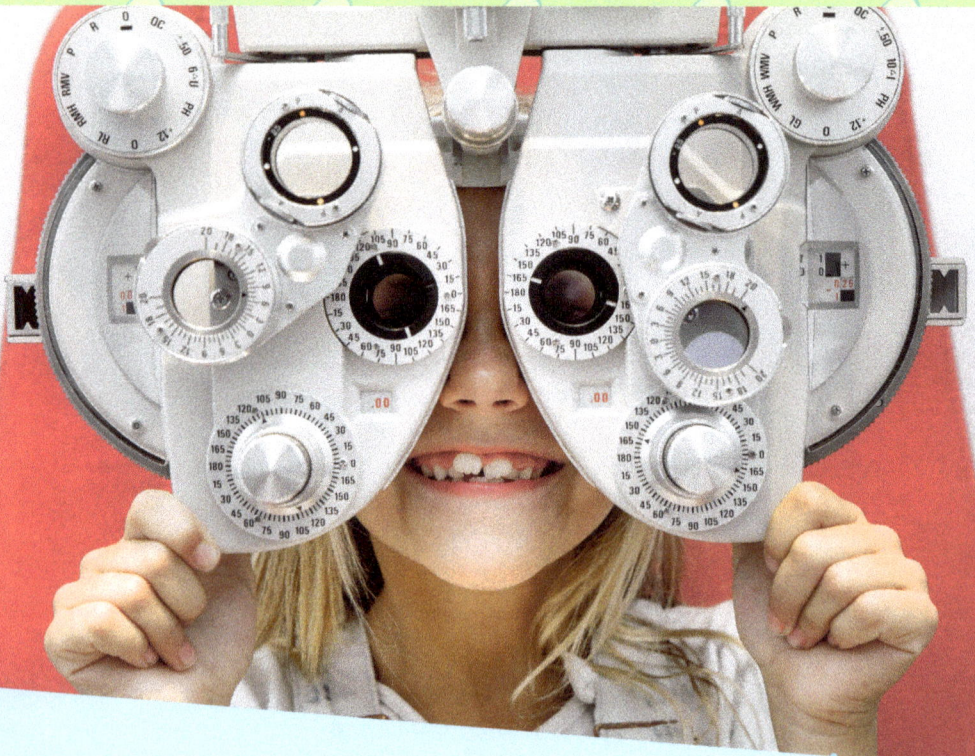

Vision Care Tip 1:
Having Regular Eye Exams

An eye exam shows whether your eyes are healthy and your vision is normal. It takes less than an hour. It may be uncomfortable at times, but it is not painful.

You may be asked to read letters off a chart from far away. Sometimes special cameras will take pictures of the inside of your eye. These tools help eye doctors **diagnose** and care for eye conditions.

KEY WORD

Diagnose: find out if someone has a medical condition.

Children should have their first eye exam at age three.

Vision Care Tip 2: Looking Away From the Screen

Many children and teens spend a lot of time looking at screens. This can lead to becoming nearsighted. That means you cannot see things unless they are very close.

To help stop this from happening, look away from the screen every 20 minutes. Then focus on an object 20 feet away from you for 20 seconds.

Vision Care Tip 3: Eating Vision-Healthy Foods

Vitamins and minerals are important **nutrients** your body needs to stay healthy. Different foods have different vitamins and minerals. Some foods have vitamins and minerals that help keep your vision healthy. Make sure to eat lots of these.

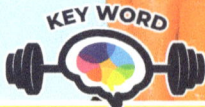

KEY WORD

Nutrients: something in food that help people, animals, and plants live and grow.

Vision-Healthy Foods

- Carrots
- Strawberries
- Kale
- Almonds
- Sunflower seeds
- Salmon
- Beans
- Eggs
- Oranges
- Bell peppers
- Tomatoes
- Tuna
- Spinach
- Peas
- Peaches
- Grapefruits

Quiz

Test your knowledge of vision loss by answering the following questions. The questions are based on what you have read in this book. The answers are listed on the bottom of the next page.

1 Does vision loss always affect both eyes?

2 How do people read braille?

3 What percentage of vision loss can be prevented or helped?

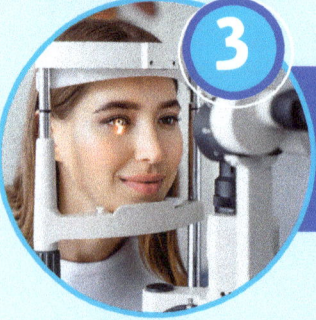

4 Where was the first school for the blind?

5 Erik Weihenmayer was the first blind person to reach the top of what mountain?

6 How long does an eye exam take?

Explore Other Level 3 Readers.

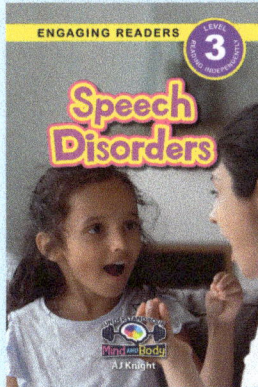

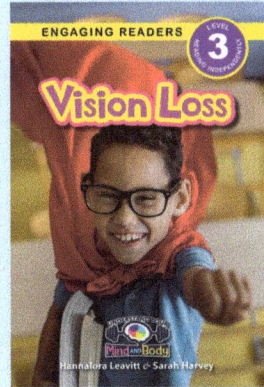

ENGAGING READERS — LEVEL 3

ADHD
AJ Knight

Anxiety
Adelaide Wilder

Asthma
Sarah Harvey

Body Image
Adelaide Wilder

Dyslexia
Sarah Harvey

Diabetes
Kit Caudron-Robinson

Obesity
Kit Caudron-Robinson

Speech Disorders
AJ Knight

Vision Loss
Hannalora Leavitt & Sarah Harvey

Visit www.engagebooks.com/readers

www.ingramcontent.com/pod-product-compliance
Lightning Source LLC
Chambersburg PA
CBHW051241020426
42331CB00016B/3472